THE ENGLISH ASSOCIATION

Presidential Address

1973

WALTER DE LA MARE

BY

LORD DAVID CECIL

C.H.

JULY 1973

Oxford University Press, Ely House, London W. 1

GLASGOW NEW YORK TORONTO MELBOURNE WELLINGTON
CAPE TOWN IBADAN NAIROBI DAR ES SALAAM LUSAKA ADDIS ABABA
DELHI BOMBAY CALCUTTA MADRAS KARACHI LAHORE DACCA
KUALA LUMPUR SINGAPORE HONG KONG TOKYO

ISBN 0 19 721487 8

PRINTED IN GREAT BRITAIN

WALTER DE LA MARE

Ladies and Gentlemen

I MUST begin by saying how pleased I am to be here. My first
reason is because I feel it a deeply gratifying honour to have been
invited to be President of the English Association; so distinguished
a Society and one in which my predecessors have been such eminent
men. My second reason is that it gives me an opportunity to speak
about Walter de la Mare, born one hundred years ago this year; de
la Mare is an author whose work has had a special appeal for me
ever since I was in my teens. We each, I think, have authors who
speak to us, as it were, on a private line, whose vision of reality has
for us a particular and intimate significance: and to whom, therefore,
we owe a particular debt. For me de la Mare is one of these few
authors. I am grateful this afternoon to have the opportunity pub-
licly to acknowledge my debt.

Walter de la Mare—it is a beautiful and unusual name! So also
are the works of its owner. From 1902 to 1956 he wrote steadily in
prose and verse but never produced anything that could possibly be
mistaken for the work of any other author. This is not to say he was
a 'revolutionary' writer. On the contrary, he is our last great writer
in the original romantic tradition. Like Keats, like Wordsworth, like
Coleridge, he is concerned with the inner life, the inner dream of
rapture or sadness or terror; and, as with them, his sense of these
things finds expression in images drawn from folk-tale and romance,
or from a close and loving observation of visible nature. In the
romantic fashion too he looks back to childhood as a period when
spiritual experience was strongest and purest; and, above all, his
writing is soaked in that typical romantic emotion mingling aspira-
tion and despair, which comes from a sense of the poignant contrast
between the splendour of man's dreams and the disillusioning sadness
of his experience in this imperfect and transient existence. Tech-
nically, too, he is a romantic in the traditional mode with his
subtle lyrical rhythms that recall Poe and Christina Rossetti, and
his diction that now looks back to nursery rhymes and now to the
richly embroidered manner of Keats and Coleridge. Equally does his
prose reveal its ancestors: Emily Brontë has left her mark on his
matter and Henry James on his manner.

To be traditional, however, does not mean to be unoriginal. One
can describe a scene as 'de la Maraish' in the same way as one can
describe one as Hardyish or Dickensian. For he is one of those rare
writers who has created a world all his own. What are its distin-
guishing characteristics? They are diverse and incongruous. Often,
and especially in his prose works, the cast and setting are homely;

children, old maids and bachelors, old-fashioned servants, the keepers of lodging houses and small shops, living in placid country towns or tranquil rural cottages. But he also introduces us to witches and mermaids and elves, to mouldering Gothic castles and Arabian deserts and caves of pearl and coral hidden in the depths of the ocean. And even his homely characters and scenes have something queer about them. The houses are secret and irregular, full of dark nooks and dusty accumulated junk; quaint ornaments, forgotten books, dim portraits. The children are odd children, with their demure manners and solemn eyes and heads buzzing with fancies; the bachelors and old maids are solitary and eccentric, the landladies and shopkeepers are as full of grotesque idiosyncrasy as the personages of Dickens. There is a noticeable touch of Dickens in de la Mare's imagination. Yet his world is not like that of Dickens. Dickens's world, for all its oddness, is life-size, solid, and earthbound. That of de la Mare is elfin, haunted, gossamer, and with a curious bias towards the miniature. Its creator is fascinated by anything small. His most sustained work, *The Memoirs of a Midget*, has for heroine a woman two feet high; one of his most typical stories, *At First Sight*, tells of a young man who, owing to some physical disability, cannot raise his eyes above the level of his knee. For the rest, his scene is largely peopled by children, birds—especially wrens and robins—moths, ants, glow-worms, dewdrops, and snowflakes.

> What lovely things
>   Thy hand hath made:
> The smooth-plumed bird
>   In its emerald shade,
> The seed of the grass,
>   The speck of stone
> Which the wayfaring ant
>   Stirs—and hastes on!

This stanza is highly characteristic of its author. When de la Mare wishes to praise God for the beauty of his creation, he chooses microscopic examples; a seed of grass, a speck of stone. Not that his feeling for beauty is confined to the minute. On the contrary, it shimmers over his whole picture of the world. But it is always in character with the rest of his genius, always an elfin beauty; the beauty of his heroines with their pale narrow faces, and slanting sloe-black eyes; of his overgrown gardens, heavy with the scent of lime leaf and honeysuckle; of the strange radiant birds—these are a strikingly characteristic expression of his imagination—which come now and again, no one knows from where, to sweep with wild call across his landscape; of his lonely country churchyards, where the eye moves upwards from mossy gravestone to contemplate the moonlit night skies or shadowy twilights, which provide the setting for so many of his scenes. There is very little full sunlight in de la Mare's world.

This goes to make its atmosphere eerie; and for all its homeliness, de la Mare's world is an eerie place. Elves and mermaids are eerie things if taken seriously. De la Mare takes them with complete seriousness. Moreover, there are more sinister things than elves in his universe. The magic he evokes is not a comfortable magic. It disquiets the spirit as the supernatural would if we came across it in real life. Even when it is benevolent, it is convincingly genuine, and as such, disturbing to the sense of security. But often it is far from benevolent. Though again and again he uses some nursery tale theme, it is often in such a way as to disclose the element of terror latent in it. He has for instance given us several variations on what may be called the 'Red Riding Hood' theme—that of innocent childhood pursued by malignant, inhuman forces—but, in his variations, more often than not the wolf gets his way. In *Henry Brocken* he shows us a glimpse of the Sleeping Beauty's palace; but what an uncanny place it is with its population of sleepers lying eternally young amid crumbling stonework and curtained over by overgrown weed and creeper and spiders' webs, all glimmering in the moonlight! There is a touch of nightmare in it. As for those tales like *Seaton's Aunt* or *Out of the Deep* in which he deliberately treats of black magic, they communicate to us the immediate inexplicable horror of a very bad nightmare. Indeed, he does not need magic to stir a sense of nightmare. It breathes from such realistic tales as *An Ideal Craftsman* with its sinister little boy so cool to dispose of a corpse, or *Missing*, the tale of a possible undiscovered murder, related in a shabby London teashop under the brooding oppressive half-light of a thunderous summer afternoon. A nightmare is a dream. The outstanding quality of de la Mare's work is its dreamlike quality. His world is as enigmatic as that of a dream: it has also a dream's intensity.

Midgets and ghostliness, homeliness and dream—such are the surface features of de la Mare's world. They are, however, far from being its only features. If they were, his work would not be so memorable. De la Mare is, in the truest sense of a misused overworked word, a symbolist. The outer world he shows us is the expression of an inner world, the external drama, the incarnation of an internal drama: and that internal drama is concerned with some of the profoundest and most critical issues that confront the human soul. Indeed, he is occupied with nothing less than the ultimate significance of experience. What does life mean? he asks. What is the nature of the universe that we see around us? He has said that *The Listeners*, his most famous poem, was about man confronting the universe. It is the subject of a great many other of his poems as well.

Not that he comes to any hard and fast conclusions as a result of his contemplations. Life remained mysterious to him right up to the day of his death. But he was sure of certain things about it: above all that it was not what it might appear at a superficial glance. He was filled with a sense of the fleetingness, of the insubstantiality of what looked solid and permanent. Has the world, indeed, any objective existence? he wonders. Is it not merely a reflection of our own minds altering according to the mood and character of the observer? To de la Mare, as to Blake, what appeared to one man to be a thistle, to another might be a grey-headed old man. Who can say with certainty which is right? 'It seemed to him', so he says of one of his child heroes, '. . . almost as if the world was only in his mind, almost as if it was the panorama of a dream.'

Almost—the word is important. For de la Mare did not in fact take a wholly objective view of experience. Although he never ceased to question, he had a faith. There was a streak of mysticism in de la Mare. His central conviction seemed to be that behind the insubstantial ephemeral world of matter that we perceive through our senses, lies an eternal universe of spiritual forces of which that material world is but the temporary incarnation. He is much concerned with death; but less as a finality, than as the possible gateway to another mode of existence. Not that he is blind to the fact of physical dissolution. With memorable force he describes Miss M.'s horror on finding a mole's carcase crawling with maggots. 'So this is what lies in wait; this is how things are!' she cries in a flash of realization. But neither to her nor to her creator does such a spectacle seem proof of the annihilation of the soul. De la Mare has had intimations from the spiritual world too vivid for him to doubt its existence for long.

Here he reminds us of Emily Brontë. The moral of *The Memoirs of a Midget* recalls that of *Wuthering Heights*, in its suggestion that a human being only finds true fulfilment in union with another human being who is his or her spiritual affinity, and that if he fails to achieve this union in life, he strives for it after death. Mr. Anon comes from the grave to claim Miss M. in the same way as Cathy comes back to claim Heathcliffe. But de la Mare's interpretation of reality is more tentative than Emily Brontë's. He makes less attempt to map the spiritual universe of which he is conscious. For him it remains obscure, a dark mysterious place in which he dimly perceives benevolent and malignant forces eternally at war with each other. But which is the most powerful he does not say; because, so one guesses, he does not know. In *The Memoirs of a Midget* good prevails. Miss M. through her own errors has caused the death of her spiritual affinity, Mr. Anon. But she has expiated her sin, so that at the end the spirit of Mr. Anon is able to take her to himself. In *Seaton's Aunt*, on the other hand, evil is victorious. Wretched little Seaton has done no harm; yet this cannot save him from destruction at the hands of those demonic powers of which his aunt is the horrible instrument. Of one thing de la Mare does seem certain. Man should realize the spiritual nature of the universe, he must never forget that the material world is not the only world; or he will lay his soul open to the attack of the forces of destruction who are always lying in wait for him. The hero of *The Return*, because he has been content to live a wholly superficial and material life, creates, as it were, a spiritual vacuum in himself. In consequence the soul of a wicked and miserable suicide, many years dead, takes up its habitation within him. Miss M. nearly wrecks her life because she allows her infatuation with the fickle and worldly Fanny to blind her to the fact that true spiritual fulfilment can only come from her union with Mr. Anon.

De la Mare exhibits his vision most fully in these prose works. In his poems he rather pin-points some aspect of it; loving delight in nature, dream of beauty or of terror, sense of the transience of all things mortal, apprehension of death, bewilderment at the dark riddle of existence. Most of these are not reassuring sentiments. De la Mare is not a reassuring writer. Yet he is not a disheartening one. For one thing, his response to the beautiful is too intense. Neither terror nor doubt nor sadness can quench his delight in it; and this is no cool, inhuman, aesthete's delight. Always he responds to beauty with a fresh and human tenderness. Indeed, de la Mare's quality of feeling is unique by reason of its blend of responsiveness on one hand with disillusionment on the other. Though he feels that beauty crumbles, and even love itself dies—'alas, the old often lose their power to love', he laments in *The Old Men*—yet this realization cannot prevent his whole nature welling out in joy as he watches the moths and smells the roses and looks out on a winter morning to see the earth radiant under its mantle of new-fallen snow.

> Why hath the rose faded and fallen, yet these eyes have not
>   seen?
> Why hath the bird sung shrill in the tree—and this mind deaf
>   and cold?
> Why have the rains of summer veiled her flowers with their
>   sheen
>   And this black heart untold?

> Here is calm Autumn now, the woodlands quake,
> And, where this splendour of death lies under the tread,
> The spectre of frost will stalk, and a silence make,
>   And snow's white shroud be spread.

> O self! O self! Wake from thy common sleep!
> Fling off the destroyer's net. He hath blinded and bound thee
> In nakedness sit; pierce thy stagnation, and weep;
>   Or corrupt in thy grave—all Heaven around thee.

Gratitude showed itself in these last lines; and this is typical of de la Mare. His sense that life is brief and sometimes horrifying does not turn him against it; he is too grateful for the exquisite moments it has brought him. He feels he owes it to life to enjoy these to the full.

> Leave this vain questioning. Is not sweet the rose?
> Sings not the wild bird ere to rest he goes?
> Hath not in miracle brave June returned?
> Burns not her beauty as of old it burned?
>   O foolish one to roam
>   So far in thine own mind away from home!

Moreover, for him man's delight in the created world somehow sanctifies it; so that it acts as an antidote against his sense of horror and of death.

> Look thy last on all things lovely,
> Every hour. Let no night
> Seal thy sense in deathly slumber
>   Till to delight
> Thou have paid thy utmost blessing;
> Since that all things thou wouldst praise
> Beauty took from those who loved them
>   In other days.

Beauty, for de la Mare as for Congreve's Mirabel is, at least in part, the lover's gift; we make the rose lovelier by admiring it. Yet its beauty is not wholly in the eyes of the beholder. Here de la Mare's mysticism comes in. For him transient material beauty is the image of an eternal spiritual beauty.

> When music sounds, all that I was I am
> Ere to those haunts of brooding dust I came.

It is this glimpse of some platonic vision of the eternal beauty which saves de la Mare from dust-and-ashes pessimism, and enables him to remain responsive while facing the fact that in this world everything, in the end, fades and passes.

De la Mare arrived at his view of life early and kept it unchanged. The tone of his later work differs from that of his early, for, as with so many other poets, the visionary power of youth faded, and with it the lyrical impulse movement which gave it a voice. The later de la Mare is less of a visionary seer, more of a smiling ruminative sage. His last long work, *Winged Chariot*, shows him employing a rambling, amiable, conversational mode of expression, in which he states his views overtly rather than incarnating them in a brief, imaginative flight. But his preoccupations, his reactions, remain unaltered: and the most sustained imaginative effort of his old age, *The Traveller*, is apparently a symbolic image of man's life, more especially a poet's life, which reveals him as concerned with the just same things as was his early work; man's bewilderment in face of a mysterious universe, his visionary dreams of supernatural beauty and supernatural terror, his sense of precariousness and transience, his fitful, radiant intimations of spiritual unity with a benignant universe.

De la Mare's imagined world then is of much deeper and more serious significance than its delicate and freakish surface might lead one to expect. His ghosts and hauntings, for instance, are no mere device to awaken pleasing shudders, but symbols of his belief in the soul's immortality, its capacity to influence events in this world even after death. It is from no whim either that he chooses so often to show us his story through the eyes of a child or a childish grown-up person. Living so largely in the imagination as they do, such people are less likely, than are the mature and active, to be cheated into thinking that the material world is the only reality. They stand, as it were, in the no man's land between the regions of matter and spirit, aware of both and thus able to see each in its true proportion. Though they may not grasp the superficial facts of worldly events as accurately and fully as a normal adult would, yet, so de la Mare suggests, they are nearer to the heart of their ultimate significance. His whimsical mixture of the homely and the magical, too, expresses his profound sense that supernatural forces are at work everywhere, even in the most unexpected quarters. Nor does the dream-like atmosphere of his world indicate any wish to 'escape' from reality. On the contrary, reality as de la Mare conceives it is of the nature of dream and most accurately portrayed in a dream-like mode. Indeed, dreams themselves are as much or as little real as anything else in life. Waking experience is not different in kind from that known in sleep; it is just as inexplicable and insubstantial, just as subjective. 'We are such stuff as dreams are made on'—Shakespeare's line is often on de la Mare's lips. No wonder: it sums up his principal conviction about the nature of human existence; it is the centre of his vision of life.

An unusual vision to express! And de la Mare has taken pains to fashion unusual and appropriate forms for it. For his prose tales he employs a complex, highly orchestrated style, rich with imagery, freaked with archaic words and poetical turns of speech, and moving in slow, winding, incantatory rhythms: and even when, his prose style is relatively simple, his method of narration is not. Here it is we see the influence of Henry James. There is very little straight-forward exposition or direct statement in these stories: the events of the drama are conveyed to us mainly by hint and suggestion and implication, made still more elusive by the crepuscular haze in which de la Mare veils his scene in order to induce in the reader an appropriate spellbound mood. He does not always succeed. Sometimes he overdoes the subtlety, with the result that the story is too obscure for the reader to grasp its meaning. He also can fail to do justice to the natural and supernatural aspects of his world. This problem inevitably faces writers whose stories move on two planes of reality. How are they to make both equally convincing? Most come to grief over the supernatural. We believe in the story till the magic begins. Consider E. M. Forster's *Story of a Panic* for instance. The contemporary English people on their holiday abroad are as real as possible. The Great God Pan, on the other hand, is very unreal, a limp puppet from the faded raree-show of the nineties. When de la Mare fails, it is in the opposite way to E. M. Forster. The ghostly happenings in a story like *Crewe* are disturbingly convincing, but its picture of the material world is too ethereal and bewitched to seem genuinely material.

His poetry is strong and weak in the same way as his prose. Its outstanding characteristic is its rhythm, where, by employing a number of extra syllables, cunning varied in stress over a basically simple movement, he achieves extraordinary effects of lightness and subtlety.

> Green Mistletoe!
> Oh, I remember now
> A dell of snow,
> Frost on the bough;
> None there but I:
> Snow, snow, and a wintry sky.
>
> None there but I,
> And footprints one by one,
> Zigzaggedly,
> Where I had run;
> Where shrill and powdery
> A robin sat in the tree.
>
> And he whistled sweet;
> And I in the crusted snow
> With snow-clubbed feet
> Jigged to and fro,
> Till, from the day,
> The rose-light ebbed away.

And the robin flew
Into the air, the air,
The white mist through;
And small and rare
The night-frost fell
Into the calm and misty dell.

And the dusk gathered low,
And the silver moon and stars
On the frozen snow
Drew taper bars,
Kindled winking fires
In the hooded briers.

And the sprawling Bear
Growled deep in the sky;
And Orion's hair
Streamed sparkling by:
But the North sighed low:
'Snow, snow, more snow!'

De la Mare's characteristic diction, too, is light and simple, though
enriched by occasional romantic and archaic phrases. But though
his instrument can achieve the exquisite, it is limited in range. De la
Mare seems to have realized this. In *The Traveller* he changes over
to a heavier diction and slower movement, strongly influenced by
Shakespeare. Alas, de la Mare's muse lacks the drive and mental
energy to handle such a mode! Pictures and those alike are obscured
by too much imagery; the movement of the poem is slack and
fatigued. Some of his lyrics, too, suffer from a sort of verbal fatigue.
He overworks his symbols. 'Rose', 'Twilight', 'Dream', 'Moon'—in his
later work especially these are often clichés. It is not that he has
ceased to feel poetically. We get the impression that de la Mare's
fresh response to experience never failed him: nor the urge to write
which it created. But his technical equipment, beautiful and accom-
plished in its way, was yet sometimes inadequate to his inspiration.
He can give us the impression that a genuine mood has inspired him
to sing in a certain rhythm: but he furnishes out the rhythm with
stock phrases. Altogether, there is a disproportion between his mind
and imagination, on the one hand, and his gift of expression, on the
other. His imaginative vision is on a more majestic scale than his
technical gift. For this reason he soars highest on short flights, is at
his best in lyrics and short stories. There is quite enough matter to
fill his longer works like *The Memoirs of a Midget* and *The Traveller*,
but he has not the manner to sustain such a length.

No—de la Mare's is a perilous kind of art: and only now and
again does he practice it with complete success. But these rare

successes are unique and profoundly impressive. For, in them, he has created a universe which does include the material and the spiritual world and keeps the balance between them. No one has ever described certain phases of the English scene with his particular evocative vividness—drowsy evenings in rural summer, snowy winter twilight: and he can draw character, especially child character with wonderfully intimate insight. As for his command over the world of dream and spirit, it is unsurpassed in literature. He has a Coleridge-like faculty for giving a local habitation and a name to those basic nameless terrors and ecstasies and bewilderments which lurk far below the level of the conscious mind. It does not matter if we do not accept his interpretation of these phenomena. The rationalist may admire these beautiful enigmatic disquieting works simply for the true picture they give of the movements of the subconscious mind. Understood, as de la Mare intends us to understand them, they reveal surely a penetration into the spiritual regions of man's experience deeper than is to be found in the work of any other author of his time.